FOREX BIBLE

# *FOREX*

# *BIBLE*

 FOREX BIBLE

 FOREX BIBLE

# INDEX

Chapter 1: What the stock market is all about

Chapter 2: Stock Market Trends

Chapter 3: An Introduction to Forex

Chapter 4: Understanding Currency Conversion

Chapter 5: Understanding Statistics

Chapter 6: Currency volatility and market expectations

Devaluation and revaluation

Chapter 7: Aspects of Trade

The market makers and the sale of short circuits

Chapter 8: Risk Management

Chapter 9: Fashion words

Chapter 10: Negotiation Options for Experts

Chapter 11: Other Trading Options

Chapter 12: In Review

Chapter 13: A Final Choice

 FOREX BIBLE

 FOREX BIBLE

# Chapter 1: What the stock market is all about

In any lucrative business or enterprise, preparation and prior knowledge are the keys to success. Without this kind of knowledge, the attempt to make a profitable financial decision can only end in disaster and failure, regardless of your level of motivation and determination or the amount of money you plan to invest.

In the stock market, this rule applies to the umpteenth degree, since you are investing your own money in what could be considered a high risk bet, and you are playing with fire if you do not have at least a

general knowledge of how it works. Since having experience in any area is useful in guiding you through a path in that particular region, the more solid your investment knowledge base, the more likely you will benefit from any attempt to trade in the open market.

In many ways, trading on the stock exchange can be compared to driving - you don't need to be an expert to drive a car, although you are expected to have some prior knowledge of basic traffic laws, including traffic violations, safety regulations and other legal vehicle violations, which are learned either through specific studies and courses or even through some form of simple exposure (such as the years you've spent riding with your parents and others you've driven for years). You should be able to understand the basic tools used to navigate a car (where the brake

pedal is in front of the accelerator, and how to use the rearview mirror, for example), even if you have never touched a steering wheel.

The same thing happens when you enter the world of the stock market. Although you don't need to know all the terminology (at first you won't be selling short or determining your own long and short positions, so you don't have to fully understand these references, although you should be aware of them), you certainly must be versed in the basic functionality of trading stocks, bonds, stocks and other commodities. And just like someone who is behind the wheel of a car and getting ready to touch the accelerator pedal for the first time, you should start cautiously and work slowly. A first-time driver will set the mirrors to his liking, then start the car, look for interfering traffic and release the accelerator pedal, never step on it, and test the engine as you walk out the door on the first attempt. Similarly, when you select your first investment, you should choose something stable with few fluctuations and not invest a large sum of money in this first venture.

When a person is learning to drive, they will be accompanied by a more experienced person who will help them make better driving decisions and offer corrections that will help them learn to drive the car more efficiently. In the stock market, there are stockbrokers and other experts who can provide you with information and advice to help you develop your knowledge of the raw materials you are interested in, essentially "guiding" you to better buying and selling decisions in the stock market.

 FOREX BIBLE

You could spend hours and hours researching the stock market and its functionality, learning how to get involved in trading and who to contact to get into the game, especially if your interest is in the Foreign Exchange Market, which goes well beyond the level of complication of the national stock market. However, in this book, you will find all the basic information you need to begin the path to commercial success. All the work and research has been done by you, collecting the data and knowledge from a single source from which you can get enough information to make you a successful trader in the open market. All you have to do is read to gain knowledge and wisdom, passed on step by step that will lead you to an intoxicating level of success. In this Ebook, you will find all the useful information, all gathered in one source for

 FOREX BIBLE

easy reference.

## How the investment works

Any time you're going to put your money in a fund; it's a good idea to start by understanding what you're buying. The stock market is a complicated entity, and doing minimal business in trading requires a fair amount of basic knowledge, as well as understanding and acceptance of the high risk factor. The more you know beforehand about the functionality of the system, the less likely it is to be affected, resulting in a devastating loss.

First, and probably most importantly in the business of trading, you must understand what the actions really are. When you buy or

 FOREX BIBLE

sell a stock in the open market, you should be aware that you are dealing with real objects, not pieces of paper; you are buying and selling real parts of a particular company, its product, or some other commodity.

Owning a "stock" means that you have actually purchased the company or product in question and have become a partial owner of that commodity. Of course, you could be one of the millions of shareholders, since most companies and products are divided into tiny pieces altogether, but you are still considered an investor in that company or product until you sell your shares.

Think of it as if you were paying for a tank of gasoline in the car your parents bought you to drive. You may even have bought the oil filter that has been put in the car, and you

may feel that this investment makes you a co-owner. However, if we look at the total cost of the car, we have actually contributed very little to that amount. However, as long as you continue to invest in the car's gasoline and take care of the maintenance needs, you can claim partial ownership of the car.

Because the value of a company and its products or services can fluctuate continuously, the value of the shares you own will not be the same day to day and can sometimes even change every hour. When the price per share goes down and is considered low, it's an ideal time to buy. This is the least expensive way to start your business, and working with a stockbroker will allow you to learn more about which stocks are ripe for purchase at any given time.

By doing so, you become a shareholder, and the value of your properties will fluctuate from day to day. Your bet (and hope!) is that the value of the company or product you have invested in will increase or bounce back from the low price at which you made your purchase. This is the goal of all traders and means that your shares will be more valuable.

As the value of your securities increases, so does your net worth. When the price of the shares you own reaches a high point, it's time to sell, making a profit on your original investment. Ideally, you will always sell your shares for a price reasonably higher than the purchase amount and should never sell when the current value of the shares is below their initial purchase price. It is important to make sure that you do not suffer a net loss on purpose, as there are many occasions when you may be forced to suffer a loss.

For example, if you buy shares of a company for twenty dollars each, you should never sell them for eighteen dollars each. If possible, you want to wait until each of them is worth perhaps forty dollars, essentially doubling your money. Of course, this is just an example, and not all stocks will double in value, but the illustration is significant.

There are other, more complex ways of investing in the stock market. However, like learning to ride a bicycle, you won't want to make your first attempt without training wheels.

## Making Decisions in the Beginning

Let's go back to driving as a reference. When you start driving for the first time, you will not enter the road and will take the car at speeds of sixty and seventy miles per hour. Instead, you will remain in residential areas or at least on the access road; where there is less pressure to maintain such a high speed. In the stock market, you will also want to stay away from any expensive stock or extremely volatile investments until you feel very comfortable with the negotiation process.

There are small investment opportunities called "penny shares," which will help you test your sea legs and understand how the

 FOREX BIBLE

stock market works before investing large sums of money and risking a large financial loss. These particular stocks literally cost cents or small amounts in dollars and usually only fluctuate in fractions of a cent on a given day, making them extremely safe for those just starting out.

Once you master it and can better judge market trends, you'll be able to move comfortably into the more complicated and adventurous areas of the market. It's like removing your training wheels from your bike or entering the highway for the first time at an hour of the day when there's no traffic to deal with.

Keep in mind that just as you can fall off your bike once or twice and end up with some scratches and bruises, you can lose money on an investment here and there. This is very typical, and investing in the stock market is very much like betting. In poker, you can't expect to win all the cards, and the same thing happens in the investment world. Learning to observe market trends, however, is similar to observing other cars as you join the traffic and determining the correct speed and proximity to other cars for optimal safety. This diligent study can help you improve your statistics drastically in no time.

 FOREX BIBLE

# Chapter 2: Stock Market Trends

Understanding stock market trends can make your job of making money in the market much simpler. Conversely, if you know little or nothing about these trends you can cause serious losses.

**Bulls and Bears**

As you delve deeper into the market and learn more about how it works, you will begin to hear certain terms about marketing trends that seem to repeat themselves over and over again. Market trends are variable and volatile, both daily and over long periods of time. In the past, for example, the United States has had devastating stock market crashes, but because of the freedom of a capitalist society, the U.S. economy has always rebounded.

What does it mean for the market or for a particular stock to recover? Assuming that the value of a company or its stock has plummeted to a level that seems irrecoverable, leaving it virtually worthless, it may feel as if that company is in danger of bankruptcy and falls entirely outside the reach of free trade markets. Suddenly, however, the founder of that company may introduce a new product that drives consumers crazy. Everyone wants one, and this product may be scarce at the time of introduction, causing a race to the shelves of department stores.

When this happens, the law of supply and demand will take over, making the company valuable again. The stock price of that company will recover, and the resulting gain in value would be considered a rebound - a return to the original (or better) state before the devastating loss.

Market trends go up or down, and there are specific references to strong changes in market values that you may hear frequently. If several different areas of the market are in a sharp decline, with values falling rapidly (perhaps even ten or twenty percent in a few days), it is called a bear market. You may remember this reference as if you were in the extremely dangerous position of being chased by a bear - if you are in possession of several stocks or other commodities worth a

good sum, you have a serious chance of losing a large amount of value which could translate into a loss of net value if you decide to sell, and it can be a similar, very dangerous situation.

Your best bet in these cases is to sell before prices fall below your original purchase price or hold stocks until the market rebounds. However, when the bear market reaches a low point, it may be an ideal time to enter the game, as it is rare for prices to fall below this point. So, if you patiently wait for the recovery or rebound of the market, you can make a lot of money from a bear market. These options will be discussed further in later chapters.

At the same time, a bull market is a strong general uptrend for many stocks. It can be

compared to the running of bulls in Pamplona, Spain, every year. You are safer if you are at home when the race occurs, and for the same reason, if you have shares during a bull market, you are in a privileged position to increase your net value and sell your shares, earning a large amount of money. This is another idea that will be explored in more detail later in this Ebook.

## Market Perspectives

By taking note of several changes in the state of the different stock options available, you will learn to detect early market trends, which will give you a clue about the future of a particular commodity, and this can only increase your chances of profitability. Prediction is an important part of the game when working in the stock market, as you

can never be completely sure in which direction the market will move at any given time.

However, you can make an educated guess, in the same way that a meteorologist forecasts the weather. While he or she is not right 100% of the time, the forecast is usually quite close to the actual weather result because the meteorologist is a scientist who has studied the weather trends and can pick out the details that help make that educated guess. With a little time and experience, the same level of experience and intuition can be achieved within the stock market.

Once you feel more comfortable operating in the same world as stockbrokers and day traders, and feel confident (or at least nervous or uncomfortable) in making such

important financial decisions, you may decide to move into the Forex market (more commonly known as Forex), and the goal of this book is to prepare you to trade within the limits of this more complex entity. Below, we will discuss some of the properties of Forex and how complex this entity can be compared to a standard domestic market.

The Forex market is incredibly volatile, and there are many more factors to consider when placing an order in this market than in a domestic market. The next chapter is an introduction to the exciting and somewhat terrifying world of the Forex market.

FOREX BIBLE

# Chapter 3: An Introduction to Forex

Forex is the nickname for the Forex market. In the United States, there are several branches of the stock market, each with its own name. For example, some shares are traded on the Dow Jones, others on the NASDAQ. Of course, all trading in the United States takes place on the New York Stock Exchange (NYSE). The same is true in other countries. There may be one or more different markets.

However, international trading takes place in a market called the Foreign Exchange Market, or Forex. Several countries around

the world in almost every time zone participate in Forex trading, with multiple currencies being used and stocks and commodities from all participating countries being offered for trading. Because there are so many nations and time zones involved, Forex does not function as a "business day" entity like most national stock markets. It is open for trading 24 hours a day, 5 days a week.

Of course, these extra hours intensely increase the risk factor for those of us who are human and obviously cannot monitor our investments 24 hours a day. This means that the value of your properties could plummet overnight, while you sleep, because other countries are still trading while you are in a dream world. Again, it's like a car - there are a lot of moving parts under the hood, and the fact that they can't be seen doesn't mean they don't work.

This is one of the reasons why there are several safety options, such as limit orders, which we will discuss later. This is also why it is strongly recommended that your first attempts to make money on the stock market should not be transactions taking place on the foreign exchange market, but on a standard national trading market of nine to five. In our car analogy, this would be comparable to having asked someone who has never driven or even changed the oil in a car to rebuild the engine.

**Forex Functionality**

While the functionality of Forex is the same as that of a domestic stock exchange,

commodities and prices are more volatile, and there are additional factors to consider in addition to the typical risks associated with a domestic market. You will have to deal not only with the value of your shares and your currency, but also with the foreign currencies involved in any Forex trading or exchange, as well as with the inconsistencies of values of particular goods and services across international borders. It's like driving a car with a standard transmission instead of an automatic one. On the domestic front, the work is done primarily for you, and all you have to do is navigate, like an automatic transmission. However, gear switching is very similar to having to constantly participate in currency conversion. It can distract, and certainly complicates the act of driving.

Because the financial situation of many

countries is not as secure as that of the United States, this can pose a formidable problem in determining where to invest your money and what to expect in the international market. Knowing which countries and currencies are involved in Forex can help by allowing you to more closely monitor the financial situation in the nations with which you will be interacting.

**Forex History**

When foreign trade began, it was not an international trade market. This follows from the Bretton Woods agreement of 1944, which established that foreign currencies would be pegged to the dollar, which was valued at $35 per ounce of gold. This precedent was first put into practice in 1967, when a Chicago bank refused to finance a loan to a teacher in pounds sterling. Of course, his intention was to sell the currency, which in his opinion had too high a price against the dollar, and then buy it back when the value had gone down, making a quick profit.

After 1971, when the dollar was no longer convertible into gold and the domestic market was stronger, the Bretton Woods agreement was abandoned, and the currency conversion process became more variable. This allowed for greater support in foreign markets, and the United States and Europe began a strong trading relationship. In the 1980s, market hours and usage expanded through the use of computers and technology to include Asian time zones as well. At that time, foreign exchange amounted to about $70 billion a day. Today, some twenty years later, the level of trade has skyrocketed, with trade amounting to about $1.5 trillion a day.

FOREX BIBLE

Originally, trading across international lines was more difficult, with several different currencies involved throughout Europe. Although the main players in the European market were deeply involved and veterans of international trade at the time other markets joined, there were more currencies to track - the franc, pound, lira and many more - than was reasonable. With the birth of the European Union in 1992, the foundations were put in place to create a single currency to be used in most of Europe, and the euro was finally established and put into circulation in 1999.

**Forex Today**

Although some countries have not yet

accepted the currency as their own (such as Great Britain, which still uses the pound sterling), the currency conversion process has been simplified without the large number of various currencies that were previously dealt with. Instead of dozens of currencies, the major countries trade in five: US dollars, Australian dollars, pounds sterling, the euro and the Japanese yen.

Today, the foreign exchange market is international and global. The market is open 24 hours a day, 5 days a week, to accommodate all major players' time zones. These now include most of Europe, the United States and Asian markets, especially Japan. Even Australia has joined the international trading markets, and since such nations are on the other side of the world from some of the other major players, time zones obviously must be taken into consideration.Another completely separate but perhaps more important concern with Forex trading is understanding how trading in multiple currencies works. How can the value of a stock be compared across international lines if values are expressed in two separate and non-equivalent currencies? And how are gains and losses measured when the conversion rate is constantly changing?

# Chapter 4: Understanding Currency Conversion

When you start trading Forex, you have to learn how to convert currencies and notice the difference in values, as well as how currencies are exchanged between international lines. This means studying not only domestic market trends and currency values, but also those of foreign markets.

**Working with Multiple Currencies**

Since Forex is the Foreign Exchange Market, obviously you can't expect everyone in the market to trade in U.S. dollars (and why not, you might ask, but remember that not everyone covets the U.S. dollar). With so many variables and volatile currencies being exchanged, how do you know a good buy or sell when you see one without fully knowing the value of the foreign currency?

The first step is to find a source that gives you a basic idea of the current exchange rate between your national currency and the foreign currency in question. You should do this as a basic listing for any currency you may be involved with. Of course, this will not be consistent to the penny or fraction of a particular currency over an entire business day, but at least it will have its starting point from which to start, almost like the North on a compass. These sources can be found throughout the Internet, as well as through many corridors, both online and in person.

## Currency Expression

It is also good to understand the means by which currency conversion is expressed. The comparison is usually made in a proportion known as the cross rate. In this configuration, the two currencies are listed in a XXX/AAAA ratio, with the XXX item called the base currency. The base currency is usually expressed as an integer, while the YYY position is expressed as the decimal that most closely approximates the exchange rate of the base currency. It is like referring to miles per gallon or rotations per minute in a car - a direct comparison of one to another in the form of a relationship.

 FOREX BIBLE

The smallest fraction, or decimal, in which a coin can be traded is called a pip and this is usually the degree to which a cross rate is expressed. For example, if the British pound sterling can be traded in thousandths, the currency will be expressed to the third decimal place. The US dollar is often expressed to one-hundredth of a cent (the fourth decimal place).

In an example of a cross rate expression, one US dollar may be equivalent to 117,456 Japanese yen. This ratio would be expressed as 1,000/117,456. The base currency is almost always expressed as a single unit (as in one dollar against ten dollars), and often that unit of measure is the United States dollar. Since the integer value of the number (or the large figure, as it is called) of the secondary currency, or the currency in the YYY position in terms of conversion changes so

infrequently, only the decimal part of the number is often mentioned in the foreign exchange market.

Therefore, in the above proportion, you may hear the yen quoted at 0.456, not to mention at all the total of 117 yen shown in the proportion. This is because the exchange rate can vary from 117.456 to 117.423, but not to 119.024. Experiencing a change in the large figure - the whole number ahead of the decimal - unless it is just because the number was already within a few thousandths, would represent too large a change in value for a single trading period and would be a rare occurrence that could cause the entire market to make a drastic change in one direction or another.

The most common currencies found in Forex are the US dollar, the pound sterling, the euro, the Japanese yen and the Australian dollar. In the past, there would have been many more currencies to track (such as the franc, lira or Deutsche Mark). However, with the consolidation of most of the European Forex market trading into the Euro, many currencies have been eliminated, making Forex trading for other lands less complicated.

If you buy a commodity in a particular currency, and the value of that currency falls against the U.S. dollar, you can actually make money by selling that same commodity in dollars. The same happens the other way around if the value of a foreign currency increases against the U.S. dollar. Of course, you can only take advantage of such a situation if the commodity is traded in both

currencies and in both markets in question. We will discuss this process, as well as other ways to take advantage of the Foreign Exchange Market (such as arbitrage) in more depth in future chapters.

Once you are able to discern a base value of each particular currency and its conversion rate against other currencies traded on Forex, you will be able to more closely monitor the change in currency conversion, including its inconsistency and volatility. Such ideas will not seem so "strange", and you will be aware and well informed along with the professionals. Then you will have to learn to read, understand and ultimately interpret additional market trends.

## Forex Trend

Following the charts, listening to the advice of market analysts and graphic designers, and learning how to make informed predictions will help you keep track of various marketing trends. The next chapter will explain more about the use of published statistics to predict the next move in the stock market. Will it be a clear, quiet day with little activity, or is a storm approaching with winds of change and uncertainty? How can you know what will happen to your properties the next day or even later?

Simply learning to read market trends can eliminate a great deal of natural apprehension and uncertainty for beginning traders. In fact, sometimes the best first step to entering the market is to watch programs about it or read the financial sections of the newspaper detailing trends and expected results. The next chapter will explain more about how to interpret basic statistics and trends.

 FOREX BIBLE

# Chapter 5: Understanding Statistics

You are now familiar with the workings of the stock market and understand to some extent what trading on the foreign exchange market entails. Now, you would like to know how to measure market trends in order to benefit from your open market business. We are no longer talking about penny stocks or playground games. You want real goods.

The names of the game are statistics, and the first rule is that you should be aware that there is no such thing as a safe thing in the stock market. Although you can never be 100% sure at any given time of the next move

that will be made in the market as a whole, being able to read the statistics and interpret them will put you ahead of the group in terms of "guessing" what will happen next.

Investing is very much like betting. If you can keep track of the cards that have already been played, you are more informed, statistically, about what is likely to be dealt with next, which means you can instigate with greater insight than someone who has no idea what has already been played. With the market open, if you have information about what has already happened in the last few days, months or even years, you are back in a better position to conclude more logically what will happen next. You simply learn the pattern and follow it through to the end, reaping the financial rewards.

 FOREX BIBLE

## Graphics and Graphics

Wait, you thought you were gonna have to investigate and trace the past of the market by yourself? Of course not! There are people who are paid to do that kind of work. They monitor the market by hour, day, week, month and year so that they can provide the big operators with the same knowledge mentioned above. The more an investment company knows about the market, the more money they can make. The same goes for brokers. They make money when you make money, and they want to do the best they can to make sure you make smart decisions.

The best part of this is that you have access to the same information as these VIP clients. Chartists, who are essentially market analysts who publish their findings in easy-to-read charts, produce what is known as a candlestick chart. These charts are basically a combination of a line graph and a bar graph showing the trend of various stocks, indices or other interests over a specific period of time. Therefore, you can easily determine whether the commodity is on an uptrend or is taking a recession, when the last major change occurred, and for how long the stock or bond is predicted to continue on the current trajectory.

In fact, you can find information on most commodities and their market trends for years in the past, and some even since their introduction into the open market. Using this information can help you decide if it's a good idea to buy or sell the stocks or securities you're interested in, or if it's better to expect a peak in the market trend.

## Understand market trends

It is understandable that, as economies vary, the value of different commodities may change. This is because, when an economy is strong and flourishing, a nation is richer and has more purchasing power. Along with that power comes a higher value for the items purchased. In other words, if people have more money to spend and are spending more of that money in Walmart stores, the value of shares in Walmart will multiply at a considerable rate. Therefore, shareholders become richer in terms of assets, simply because buyers are driving the market with their purchasing power. When shareholders are rich, and the value of their property increases, they continue to buy shares, which, once again, drive the economy. A strong uptrend in the stock market is an excellent signal for any economy.

However, there are also things that affect the market negatively, causing stock values to plummet. For example, war rarely has a positive effect on the stock market. On September 11, 2001, when terrorists attacked the World Trade Center in New York City, the U.S. economy collapsed enormously and the nation was threatened with depression. Some analysts were certain that it would never recover properly. The same thing typically happens every time there is an attack or act of war within a nation. However, critics proved wrong, and the United States proceeded to rebound, or recover from a bad downward trend, in a strong way. This rapid recovery was mainly because the American people continued to push and spend, forcing money and wealth

back into the economy. By observing the reaction of the stock market, you can learn to read the trends based on world events.

Oil prices also commonly affect the stock market. Especially in the foreign exchange market, you will find that trends vary depending on many current events. You will also notice that, over time, the principal value (or face value) of a currency may be purposefully revised by a nation in terms of currency conversion. This is known as devaluation, which will be discussed in more detail in the next chapter.

# Chapter 6: Currency volatility and market expectations

Volatility, or the tendency to fluctuation that can affect your earnings within the stock market, is typical within a domestic market, but even more evident and much stronger in the foreign exchange market. What factors affect the value of the Forex currency, and is there any way to control this?

**Devaluation and revaluation**

As mentioned in the previous chapter, devaluation refers to the intentional decrease in the value of a currency relative to other currencies as charged by a government entity. For example, if the U.S. dollar is worth ten units of a foreign currency that is then devalued by ten percent, the U.S. dollar is now equivalent to only nine units of the foreign currency. This makes any item purchased in foreign currency more expensive for those who trade in U.S. dollars, since the exchange rate is lower. It also makes items in the foreign country less expensive to trade in U.S. dollars.

An opposite change in value can also occur, increasing the value of the foreign currency. This is called revaluation. While it may appear that the intentional adjustment of the value of a nation's currency is to "deceive," or take an unfair advantage by making foreign products cheaper to buy and increasing the value of exports, there are regulations to prevent manipulation of exchange rates for such purposes. The IMF (International Monetary Fund) charter helps prohibit such events and enforce policy.

There are ways to take advantage of devaluation and revaluation, which will be discussed later. However, what happens when the value of a foreign currency changes due to market fluctuations rather than intentional reductions or increases by a federal government or a federal bank? What effect do appreciation and depreciation have on the stock market?

**Appreciation and Depreciation**

Depreciation can easily be related to the life of a car. As soon as you drive a new car off

 FOREX BIBLE

the lot, the value is reduced by almost half. This is extreme depreciation. However, over the next few years, the car continues to lose value at a more gradual rate. This is also considered depreciation.

Currency appreciation and depreciation are changes in the value of the currency that are driven by market forces and not by government mandate. For example, in an attempt to repay certain loans, in 1998 the Central Bank of Russia announced the next devaluation of the rouble. The exchange rate, which is currently six rubles to the US dollar, would change over a period of time to 9.5 rubles to the US dollar, a depreciation of 34%.

However, before the change, there was widespread panic in the former communist nation, and the value of the ruble fell because many people in Russia chose to trade in their securities before maturity. In just one day after the announcement, the Russian rouble depreciated by a staggering 25%.

The same type of crisis occurred in the 1920s with the collapse of the U.S. stock market. At that time, panicked across the country and people rushed to banks to withdraw unavailable cash or to trade securities and stock options that had not expired. As they ran to the bank, people caused the accident rather than escaped.

On the other side of the coin, too rapid an appreciation creates a country for inflation, or an increase in the retail value of products sold to the public based on the valuation of the coin. While it is true that inflation will occur, it can be minimally softened by using currency valuation.

The appreciation can also be related to a vehicle. Men often enjoy taking old cars and restoring them to their original beauty. By doing so, they dramatically increase the value of the vehicle or appreciate it.

The ever-changing exchange rates of currency conversion and market volatility create an inherent market risk, or a potential day-to-day loss experience due to fluctuating stock prices. There is no way to diversify this type of risk, as it will always affect the investment to some extent. However, some risks may be offset by particular types of investments or forms of investment that are safer or protected.

We will take a look at long and short positions, short sales, stop orders and other ways to protect your investments from drastic losses in additional chapters. These options include the ability to pre-set the buy or sell price of a specific commodity, as well as the use of various pre-set order levels to place orders and complete transactions.

Of course, don't be fooled into thinking you can get rid of all the possible risk factors in the market. There's always a cloud hanging over your head waiting to explode, and all it takes is a small puncture. You always have to be careful, even though the idea of playing in the stock market involves inherent danger and excitement. The next chapter will help you understand reality and what it means to balance your risk factor with a basis in reality; your ego with your identity.

# Chapter 7: Aspects of Trade

You are now versed in the functionality of the stock market and have decided that you are willing to accept the risk factors involved. However, you want to know as much as you can about how to balance that risk with smart investment options. How can you be sure that the risks you take are more likely to be rewarding in the long run than destructive?

**Long and Short**

One of the most important parts of making money in the stock market is determining

your position. The long position is basically the buying position - you are about to make a long-term commitment to owning some stocks, securities or other traded commodities. The short position, on the other hand, is the selling position - you will shortly have the same type of ownership and any liability towards it.

The best time to take the long position is when stock prices are low. This will allow you to enter the market at a reasonable price and will increase your chances of profitability as the prices of new offers rise and older investment options recover or bounce back. In fact, as others take the long position and buy at the same time as you do, this will cause the value of the securities to rise through the standard rule of supply and demand, causing the beginning of what could be a bullish market.

You can equate this with the end of the month at an auto dealership. Prices tend to fall on any car left on the lot for sale, and the dealership is more often willing to negotiate because he or she wants less inventory on the lot. Similarly, when stock prices are low, some people get scared and abandon all their properties at these low prices, thinking that their stock will never regain its value. This can only help you.

When prices are high, it's probably time to turn around and sell your shares for profit, without losing anything on unrealized profits (profits that can't be counted in liquid assets or cash because they're still invested in a volatile stock option). You should never sell for a price that is below your cost, as this result in negative net worth and a loss of

funds. You should always sell for as much profit as you feel is safe.

In other words, if you buy a stock at fifteen dollars per share, and it quickly goes up to twenty-five dollars per share, it is quite possible that you feel you could reach thirty dollars per share in a week. However, you must determine if you are willing to risk losing your already assured profits of ten dollars per share to wait that long, in case the price actually falls, so you may decide to sell at the current high price.

**The market makers and the sale of short circuits**

What if the stock value goes up incredibly high, but you didn't get into that particular

product and you don't own stock? Your first step should be to visit a market maker or make a deal with a broker for a short sale. A market maker is literally a stockbroker who buys keeps a certain amount of shares of various securities or stocks on hand, which are bought during a time when market rates are low.

The company will then turn around and sell those shares to an individual at that low price, regardless of the market rate, actually making its own market (hence the name). The person who buys from the company can immediately sell the commodities in the open market at a higher interest rate, allowing him to make an incredible amount of profit in a short period of time.

A short sale is another option for a quick

profit. In this scenario, a certain number of shares will be borrowed from a stockbroker to sell when the market value is high. Your job is to wait for the stock price to go down, buy the same amount of stock and return the stock to the broker, keeping the proceeds from the sale minus the broker's fees.

The way a car dealership works with swaps is very similar. They will buy the car from you at a very low price, then turn around and sell it on the lot for a high profit margin.

One of the most positive aspects of a short sale is that you never take possession of the stock, which means you are never in a position to lose money. Since you have sold shares at a high price, you have already benefited, and in the worst case scenario, the particular shares will not go down in price.

Instead of returning the shares to the broker from whom you borrowed them, you can simply return the amount for which they were originally purchased, along with the premium.

How can you be sure that you will not exceed the best price options or lose a good rate because you are not available to place a buy or sell order with your broker? Is there any way to put limits on your trades? Next, we'll discuss ways to protect your investments and limit your risk factors.

# Chapter 8: Risk Management

One of the most important aspects of protecting your investments is balancing your risks with collateral. There are several ways to do this, and we will discuss them in this chapter.

**Limit Orders and Risk Balance**

A limit order is a permanent amount for which you have agreed to buy or sell a particular security or other commodity. For example, you have designated your broker who will not sell X Security until its value reaches a minimum value of Y dollars. At the same time, you will not buy the same value of X Security if it exceeds a value of Z. Setting limits on the price you pay for a particular security, as well as the price you will accept to sell it, protects you and your investment in several ways.

First, you are maximizing your profits, but above all, you are avoiding the loss. Any loss that occurs with limit orders will always be an unrealized loss, or a loss that cannot be measured in cash or liquid assets. In other words, until you sell the shares and reap the net loss, it won't affect your net worth. Since you have set a limit that does not allow your commodities to be sold for less than the original cost, it is not possible for you to have a loss in your net worth. At the same time, you are also insuring at least a certain amount of profit by setting your point of sale high enough to reap that particular profit.

Another way to protect your assets is coverage. This means that you create and sell a futures contract that states that when your shares reach a certain value in the future, you will sell your shares at this predetermined price. When that price is reached, the order will be processed and the transaction completed. Of course, if you ever change your mind about a limit you have set, you can place a stop order with your broker, who designates that you no longer want to trade the specified dollar amount.

You can also buy on margin. This is very similar to short selling, but instead of borrowing stocks to sell them, you are essentially borrowing money to buy stocks on your own when the market value is down.

Then, when the value of the securities you have bought increases and you can sell for a profit, you pay off the loan and keep the excess sale, minus the broker's fees. Of course, all dealings with a broker incur a premium or commission for services rendered, and it is almost impossible to operate without a broker or broker service. However, online services are often less expensive than live brokers, but you can research to determine which is your best option.

**How do I handle a hammer saw?**

No, we don't mean anything in the garage, the bedroom or a country band. A hammer saw is a market trend that defies odds. You might think it's the "shock shock. As careful as you are when you learn to drive a car and coordinate, sometimes you can't do anything to avoid being hit from behind.

Whipsaw is a term for what happens when everything points in a specific direction in the market trend, causing you to buy (if prices look like they're going up) or sell (if they look like they're about to fall), then the opposite effect occurs.

For example, if you buy a stock at five dollars per share because the stock seems to have fallen as far as it can go and seems to be starting an uptrend, then unexpectedly, the stock plummets to one dollar per share, this is considered a hammer saw effect. If this happens to you, as it surely will if you play in the market long enough, the best thing you can do is wait. The stock will do one of two things - either dissolve completely, and the company will declare bankruptcy (this is what you don't want to happen), or it will recover, and you can choose to wait for the opportunity to make a profit or you can exit as soon as the buying rate is reached.

Hammer saws are not the end of the world, and no one can expect to earn with every purchase on the stock exchange. However, if you find that you are involved in several of these instances, you should seriously reconsider your investment options. You may be reading the signals incorrectly, or you may be choosing bad stocks. You should seek advice for any future investments you expect to make before buying more shares or securities.

Another way to reverse a bad investment like this is to proceed with a clearing transaction -

FOREX BIBLE

a buy or sell that compensates for the loss of a previous transaction. You could buy additional shares in the same company at the lowest price if you expect it to recover, or you can opt for another hot commodity that is about to explode in price, either of which will help you offset your loss. You may also sell shares of a security in which you have a large amount of unrealized gains - gains that cannot be measured in liquid assets or cash due to the increase in the value of shares and security holdings - in order to replace the lost cash value.

All of these are viable options to recover a loss, but waiting for the stock value to recover is always the first option. It prevents the loss of funds already invested, maintains the option to earn profits and reduces the risk of new investments in the market.

As you grow and learn about these various options, you'll need to feel more comfortable when you're surrounded by financial gurus and gurus who speak what sounds like gibberish, mumbling words you've never heard right or left. The next chapter will guide you through some of the meanings of the main buzzwords used in the stock market and in the international financial district.

# Chapter 9: Fashion words

Now that you know a little more about the stock market, and have decided to try your hand at investing, you should be more concerned with understanding the jargon you will hear in the trading room. Although you probably won't find yourself in the middle of a group of stockbrokers screaming on Wall Street (and these days, most of the trading is done by computer anyway), knowing that learning to talk is part of walking the road.

## Margins, spreads and other condiments

Okay, its margins, not margarines, but it

sounds very similar. To understand the stock market, especially in Forex, you need to speak not a language intended for common communication, but the language of trading. For example, when you think of a margin, for many this means a variable, such as the "margin of error" of a statistic.

However, in trading, it refers to the sum of money borrowed from a broker to buy stocks when the market is on a downward trend. Then, when the stock begins its next upside, you sell the stock at the highest price, return the margin (along with the accumulated premium) and retain the profit.

When you buy on margin, the money borrowed by the broker is called a margin account. The margin account is provisional based on the value of the shares.

Occasionally, if the value of the shares purchased falls too low for the safety margin set by the broker, the broker will request that more money be deposited into the margin account to compensate for the loss. This is called margin call.

In some trades, the market value does not come into play. For example, a forward trade is established between two people or two companies outside the open market. It involves a negotiation process and an eventual price commitment. Usually, an offer is made - the offer to buy a commodity at a specified price - and a bid or offer - the price for which the other trading entity is willing to sell the securities or other holdings. The difference between these two purchase numbers is called a spread.

If the spread cannot be reduced and eventually closed, no agreement can be reached. This agreed price is called the forward price, and all the details involved in the trading process when this type of transaction takes place are detailed in a contract and are called forward points. Generally, the forward price is indicated as available for a particular date, and if the transaction is not completed by that date (referred to as the transaction date), then the transaction must be renegotiated.

**Intermediaries, shipyards and other British terms**

One of the main foreign markets that Americans trading Forex will find is that of the British. While other terms related to the stock market will be similar due to the

common language, there are some specific terms that are very different in British trading vocabulary.

For example, in the United States, brokers who hold securities bought at low prices for the purpose of selling them to clients in a market with higher prices (so that the client can turn around and resell them for profit in the open market) are called market makers. In Britain, however, this type of investor is simply called a "jobber.

Another term you'll want to familiarize yourself with is "yard. This does not refer to a green patch of earth, a measure in inches, or even 36 of something. The term is used in reference to the amount of currency rather than its value and equals one million units of the currency in question. In other words, you

may have a dollar yard or a yen yard, and although it is the same amount of bills, coins, or any other physical currency that is used, it is not necessarily equivalent in value.

In Britain, they do not use the euro, and they do not use the US dollar. They have decided to continue using the pound sterling, a currency that has been used in the country for hundreds of years. However, Britain is currently on track to make the conversion to the euro within the next five years.

**Open and close**

In the stock market, there are several types of orders that can be placed to help protect you from making a bad investment or to limit the amount you pay for a certain security or other merchandise. For example, if you have made a bad investment and do not want to reinvest in a particular security, you must sell all the shares in that security, regardless of whether you have suffered a small loss. This action is known as closing a position. Conversely, if you do well with your investment, you could participate in a reinvestment by simply reinvesting the proceeds in additional stocks or securities.

An open order is exactly what it looks like, which means that the order remains pending until it is executed by your broker or cancelled by you as a client. A stop order would cancel any pending orders you have placed with your broker. You also have options such as One Cancels the Other Orders. These allow you to have an interest in various commodities, leaving the orders to your broker to buy them all, in case they fall at a certain price. Then, if one of them reaches this pre-established low price, your broker will follow your direction and invest your money in that particular security, followed by a cancellation of all additional orders.

When a broker gives you an estimate of the price of a particular stock or product, it is considered a quote. A quote is never completely accurate and is usually referred to as a spot price, as the value of a security can change in a few seconds. However, it is as accurate as can be expected. When you place an order, the broker then processes the execution, or termination, of that order. The actual value at which the trade is completed is called the execution price. The completion of a trade or purchase, called settlement, can also be called the execution of a trade or the placing of an order. As you can see, there are many terms to keep in mind, and we have not even begun to consider the terms used in some of the most difficult areas of the market.

Next, we'll consider some specialized and more complex trading options you can use in Forex to take advantage of market volatility and constantly changing exchange rates.

FOREX BIBLE

# Chapter 10: Negotiation Options for Experts

After spending a lot of time buying and operating both domestically and abroad, you will find that the process becomes easier and almost intuitive. You no longer have to work so hard to determine currency conversion or find the next large explosive product. It will be like a second nature to you.

So what's the next big challenge for someone operating in the open market? What keeps things from becoming monotonous and boring? First of all, there is always something new and different going on in the Foreign Exchange Market. Remember, it

works 24 hours a day, and you never know what you'll find when you wake up in the morning. However, there are several ways to take advantage of the variation in currency conversion and the time lag between markets that can affect trading values.

## Arbitration

There are some commodities that are traded in multiple currencies in multiple Forex markets. Although computers have made global communication almost as fast as lightning these days, all these markets can trade together with fairly equivalent values for the values shared between the different currencies.

However, the system is not perfect, and the

value can go up or down in one country and in one currency before the same change in value arrives across another border. Experienced traders have learned to take advantage of this lag in market trend by using a process called arbitrage. In this transaction, you buy the particular stock or security in the market with the lowest price while simultaneously selling the same in a market where the security is higher. The process is a bit complex, so let's use an example. Let's say one US dollar equals 0.5 pounds sterling, which means everything is going to be twice as expensive in pounds sterling.

Now, let's take a look at the price of a share that is traded in both markets. If they were equivalent, then the shares would be traded for two dollars in the United States and one pound in Britain. However, if something

happens and the value of the shares falls in Britain, it is six hours ahead of the US, and it is possible that this fall will not affect the US market immediately.

If the value of shares falls in Britain to 0.8 pounds, the purchase price is now below the dollar price due to currency conversion. In this case, arbitrage would take place when shares are bought on the UK market in pounds and sold on the US market in dollars, benefiting from the slow communication of the fall in the value of the shares. In effect, you will earn $.40 per share.

**Currency Conversion Volatility**

Another way to take advantage of the exchange value of each individual currency is to trade on the basis of exchange rates. What exactly is it? You should carefully observe the changing conversion rates. When a currency conversion rate changes drastically, it is time to make a change. This is very similar to arbitrage, but the area is much riskier due to the high volatility. For example, if you bought a share in the previous scenario in the US market at two dollars a share, and suddenly the pound sterling gains value, falling to a conversion of only half a pound for every two dollars, you would want to sell your shares in the British market because the value of one pound is greater and you now have greater purchasing power.

One tip to keep in mind, however, is that it is best to immediately dispose of all liquid assets in foreign currency, usually on the same day. This is called tomorrow because it takes two to three business days for the foreign currency to be delivered, and by exchanging the currency for the value of the shares on the same business day, you avoid having to receive delivery of the currency in its entirety.

# Chapter 11: Other Trading Options

In addition to the expert options described above, there are other non-traditional ways to make money in the stock market. However, when considering these options, you should consider making a career trading stocks and securities. Some types of trades are simply not for the faint of heart, and that means you must have complete motivation and an adventurous spirit to participate in these areas of the market. The chances of receiving a giant hit and experiencing a big loss multiply.

## Day Trading

Daily traders take some of the biggest risks in the market. Because day traders work with investments that change drastically in a matter of hours, they are naturally playing in the lion's den. These stocks are extremely volatile, and for most, daily trading is a quick way to lose a large amount of money. It is difficult to make a large amount of cash in this way, and it is even harder to predict the outcome of these daily stock options trading. You can't be sure of the overnight position (the net value at which a stockbroker or a day trader will open the next morning).

And in Forex, there is little room for daily trading, as the market never closes during the workweek. In these cases, the day trader has to set a time limit for going out, selling all the

shares, so that you can sleep peacefully while the world spins around and starts the next day again.

Day Trading is very dangerous and is not recommended to newcomers. In fact, it is not really recommended at all, and most people who participate in this volatile part of the industry are very experienced in trading in the open market, do not consider the risk factors carefully enough before entering this branch of the market, or have enough money they simply want to try this form of investment and do not care if they lose a good sum.

**Secondary Markets**

Secondary markets are interesting because

they are created by the government to help redistribute the money used for loans. Fannie Mae and Freddie Mac are two of the major corporations from which shares are bought in a secondary market.

That's how it works. When a person buys a house, they borrow from the bank, usually for eighty percent of the cost of the house. This is granted, and the house is purchased by the bank for the individual or family, which begins to pay the loan to the bank.

In the meantime, to ensure that the money is available in that bank for the next person who needs a mortgage loan, Fannie Mae or Freddie Mac, two entities originally established by the U.S. government, will purchase the bank loan. Therefore, the money is returned to the bank for future use.

What do these agencies do with the deficit they have acquired? They sell it. In the secondary market, they divide the loan into shares that are backed by the mortgage itself and sell those shares, recovering the money from the investors. Eventually, those securities mature, probably at the same time the original loan is paid to the bank, and investors reap the benefits of their investment with the interest earned.

Another way to take advantage of the volatility of the international stock market is to swap. It is the exchange of securities or bonds in order to take advantage of lower interest rates. For example, if a commercial entity in Britain is in possession of a security, and another in Japan is in possession of a different security, the two commodities can be traded or sold to each other in order to save on interest rates, if the bond or security currently held is held at a lower interest rate in the opposite market.

For example, let's say one company owns an "A" bond that pays only two percent interest in its current market and another that holds "B" bonds in its market at three percent interest. If bond A is actually paying three percent in the foreign market, and bond B can be charged four percent in the first market, both parties can earn more money in a bond exchange. They can mutually benefit from a sale of the securities to each other due to a gain of more interest.

If that seems confusing, then there may not be an exchange in your near future. This is processed more often between companies in

the foreign market than between individual parties, although with the right broker, it could be achieved. However, if you work on the deal, you need to know little, except that you are looking for a higher profit margin than before, and your broker will take care of the rest.

If you determine that you should have stock options as a business, you will probably decide to hire a full-time consultant for all of your financial needs, including the management of your stock holdings. In fact, when companies are big enough and have a strong enough commercial presence in the market, especially in Forex, you will find that there are entire departments dedicated to the maintenance of stock options.

# Chapter 12: In Review

After shoveling through piles of information and assimilating so much knowledge, you probably feel like you're swimming in terminology and can't remember where to start. The best way to retain knowledge is through repetition, and having a quick reference guide isn't a bad idea either. The following pages are a brief summary of the in-depth discussions of this book, allowing you to quickly refer to a subject in a binding.

**Basic Trade**

A share is an interest in an enterprise whose value varies according to the desire or need

for the goods or services of that particular enterprise. As a shareholder, you're net worth increases and decreases by taking a short position (sale) when stocks are high and a long position (buy) when prices are low. While the stock or security is in your possession, the change in value is considered an unrealized gain or loss because it cannot be measured in liquid assets (cash).

When most commodities traded on the market have a strong uptrend over a period of time, this is called an uptrend. In case the security takes a strong downtrend and continues on that path, it is called a downtrend. If such a trend is not recognized, and the value of stocks and values is fairly even, this is called flat.

## The foreign exchange market

The foreign exchange market is the stock exchange on which several countries from different time zones trade their domestic and international commodities in various currencies. The currency is the denomination or currency division used in a particular field (such as the US dollar or the euro). When multiple currencies are used, they are typically expressed as a relationship called a cross rate that shows the amount of a second currency that is equivalent to the first listed. Determining what the equivalent is known as currency translation.

Several countries in Europe have now consolidated their currencies to agree to trade the Euro (since 1999) in Forex, as it is called for short. Great Britain, which until now has

FOREX BIBLE

opted to continue using the pound sterling, also participates in international trade, as well as the United States, Japan and Australia. Each of these countries uses its own currency for standard trading purposes, with investment options in foreign currencies. Whether or not this is worthwhile depends on the currency conversion rate.

The value of a nation's currency is determined by its government and its federal bank (the Federal Reserve, better known as the FED, is the federal bank of the United States). The intentional change in the conversion rate by a government is known as valuation - devaluation is taking value and strength from the currency, and revaluation adds strength and purchasing power to the currency. If the same change in the conversion rate occurs naturally through events and market volatility, then it is called appreciation and depreciation.

## Careers in the market

Without the help of professionals, it is almost impossible to operate in the open market. Market analysts track stock market trends that affect the value of stock holdings. They use that information and basic history to help predict the outcome of different aspects of the market in the future.

Other individuals, known as chartists, create charts and graphs that interpret all the data - various numbers, statistics, percentages, etc. - on an easy-to-read candlestick chart that tracks the trends of specific products in the market.

 FOREX BIBLE

A broker is an individual or a company that helps you makes your investments. A broker can help you make smart financial decisions, help you track and place orders, and track market trends.

A market maker does the same job as a broker, except that this individual or company retains an investment in a particular variety of securities and bonds that can be short sold to a client for a lower price so that the client can earn money by immediately selling the same shares at the higher market price.

Other individuals can help with loans, allowing you to buy on margin. This implies the opposite approach: borrowing money to buy a stock or security that has a low market value, so that the customer can then resell the commodity at a higher price.

**Protecting your investments**

There are several ways to protect your investments. By placing limit orders, you guarantee in the best possible way that you will not lose money in the market and practically guarantee at least a minimum profit. However, if you change your mind about those limits, you can always place a stop order. If you leave standing instructions with your broker, they are called open orders that remain open until the transaction is executed and the order is executed.

Try to set your limit orders just above the support levels (the lowest levels of value a stock can reach) and just below the resistance level (the upper level above which it is difficult for a stock's value to rise).

Also, set a value date - a date on which you can take an average of the value of a particular product and review your options. This should be reviewed at least every six months, if you plan to retain any holdings of a particular security.

 FOREX BIBLE

# Chapter 13: A Final Choice

Although "Chapter 13" is not an appropriate way to end a financial effort, it is, in this case, one of the most important conclusions of an incredibly useful tool filled with investment advice, especially when placed at the end of a book to offer assistance to those who are threatened with bankruptcy due to poor investment decisions. There are always ways to turn around when you've started walking down the wrong path. Just like going ahead with a new car after buying a lemon that has been nothing more than a nightmare, you can reverse the direction.

Some people may spend days, months and even years trying to conquer the stock market and still fail. In some cases, it is virtually impossible for an individual to master the functionality of the market. If you can't follow market trends, then you better not make any investment decisions.

It's okay not to fit into the market. At the same time, you can still make money on investments. A last option is to create a discretionary account. This means that you sign a contract with your broker and give a sum of money to the broker to make the investment, leaving the determination of the placement of that investment to your broker. You never have to worry about making a bad investment again. In fact, in this scenario, you don't even have to follow market trends or other information that has to do with the financial investment. Your broker will simply let you know when your net worth has increased or if your assets have

FOREX BIBLE

plummeted.

Whatever choice you make regarding moving into the stock market, you don't have to worry about not having the essential information to help you get through your first trading experiences. Now, you have the basic knowledge and the essential reference guide to begin the path to success and wealth that you can access at any time.

 FOREX BIBLE

Visit our author page on Amazon and get more MENTES LIBRES!

http://amazon.com/author/menteslibres

If you wish, you can leave a comment on this book by clicking on the following link so that we can continue to grow! Thank you very much for your purchase!

https://www.amazon.com/dp/B0829DQ2VD

www.ingramcontent.com/pod-product-compliance
Lightning Source LLC
Chambersburg PA
CBHW070804220526
45466CB00002B/542